Standard Grade | General

French

General Level 2000
General Level Reading 2000
General Level Listening Transcript 2000
General Level Listening 2000

General Level 2001
General Level Reading 2001
General Level Listening Transcript 2001
General Level Listening 2001

General Level 2002
General Level Reading 2002
General Level Listening Transcript 2002
General Level Listening 2002

General Level 2003
General Level Reading 2003
General Level Listening Transcript 2003
General Level Listening 2003

General Level 2004
General Level Reading 2004
General Level Listening Transcript 2004
General Level Listening 2004

Leckie × Leckie

First exam published in 2000.

Published by Leckie & Leckie, 8 Whitehill Terrace, St. Andrews, Scotland KY16 8RN tel: 01334 475656 fax: 01334 477392
enquiries@leckieandleckie.co.uk www.leckieandleckie.co.uk

Leckie & Leckie Project Team: Andrea Collington; Peter Dennis; Bruce Ryan

ISBN 1-84372-197-X

A CIP Catalogue record for this book is available from the British Library.

Printed in Scotland by Scotprint.

Leckie & Leckie is a division of Granada Learning Limited, part of ITV plc.

Acknowledgements

Leckie & Leckie is grateful to the copyright holders, as credited, for permission to use their material. Every effort has been made to trace the copyright holders and to obtain their permission for the use of copyright material. Leckie & Leckie will gladly receive information enabling them to rectify any error or omission in subsequent editions.
Rex Features for a photograph (2003 Reading paper p 2);
Allstar Picture Library for a photograph (2003 Reading paper p 2).

The following has very generously given permission to reproduce their copyright materail free of charge:
Richard Young for a photograph (2004 Reading paper p 5).

2000 GENERAL

FOR OFFICIAL USE

G

Total

1000/402

NATIONAL QUALIFICATIONS 2000

FRIDAY, 19 MAY
G/C 9.20 AM – 10.05 AM
F/G 10.05 AM – 10.50 AM

FRENCH
STANDARD GRADE
General Level
Reading

Fill in these boxes and read what is printed below.

Full name of centre

Town

Forename(s)

Surname

Date of birth
Day Month Year

Scottish candidate number

Number of seat

When you are told to do so, open your paper and write your answers **in English** in the spaces provided.

You may use a French dictionary.

Before leaving the examination room you must give this book to the invigilator. If you do not, you may lose all the marks for this paper.

SCOTTISH QUALIFICATIONS AUTHORITY

Marks

1. You're staying with your pen friend Pascal. One day, while you're waiting for him to come home, you look through a magazine which is lying on the table.

Your attention is drawn by this article.

Le cigare le plus long

M. Felipe Mendoza a créé le cigare le plus long du monde. Il mesure 3,40 mètres de long. M. Mendoza a travaillé pendant 50 ans dans une fabrique de cigares, donc c'est un expert.

(*a*) What is special about the cigar which Mr Mendoza has made? **1**

it is the longest in the world

(*b*) What makes him an expert? **1**

he has been making them for 50 years

DO NOT WRITE IN THIS MARGIN

Marks

2. You then read an article about Grandmother's Day.

Le premier mars, pensez à votre grand'mère. Ça, c'est la fête de toutes les grand'mères:

Vous pouvez . . .
. . . lui faire un joli cadeau ou un dessin.
. . . lui envoyer une carte postale ou des fleurs.
. . . aller la voir pour parler avec elle et pour lui faire de grosses bises.

What could you do to make Grandmother's Day special? Mention **one** thing in each box. **3**

make . . . her a a present for her	
send her . . . a bunch of flowers	
visit her and . . . give her lots of kisses	

[Turn over

Marks

3. There is a short poem in the magazine.

Poème

Pensez aux enfants qui ont faim
Pensez aux enfants qui travaillent dans les champs
Pensez aux enfants qui sont malades
Pensez aux enfants qui n'ont pas de domicile
Pensez à tous ces enfants.

This poem is about some of the problems children have throughout the world. Which problems are mentioned in the poem? Tick (✓) **three** boxes. **3**

Children who . . .

are orphans	✗
are hungry	✓
don't go to school	✗
are ill	✓
are homeless	✓
work in factories	✗

DO NOT WRITE IN THIS MARGIN

Marks

4. The magazine has some articles on young people from other countries.

Abdullah

Bonjour. Je m'appelle Abdullah Ismail. J'ai huit ans. Je suis né à Penang (au nord de la Malaisie) et je suis Malais. Je suis fier et heureux. J'adore les gâteaux très sucrés, le poulet et le riz très épicé. Je bois surtout des jus de fruits, parce qu'ici ils sont très bons et naturels. J'adore l'équitation et je rêve de faire du ski. Un jour, je voudrais voyager aux Etats-Unis. Au revoir!

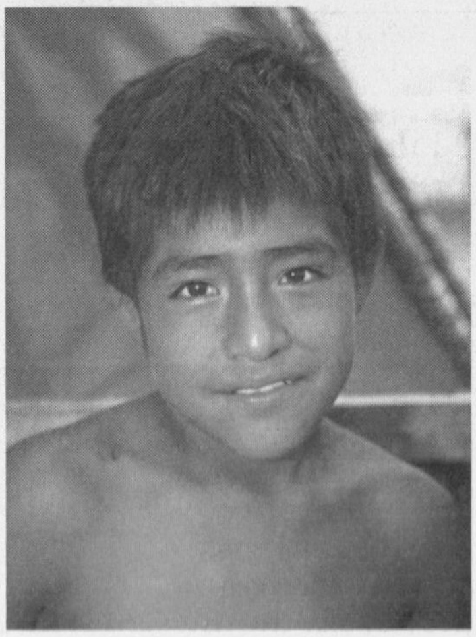

Are the following statements about Abdullah TRUE or FALSE?

Write T or F in the boxes below. **5**

He is unhappy.	F
He doesn't like sweet things.	F
He likes spicy rice.	T
He loves swimming.	F
He would like to go to the United States.	T

[Turn over

DO NOT WRITE IN THIS MARGIN

Marks

5. On the next page Abdullah talks about some customs in his country, Malaysia.

La Malaisie

En Malaisie, les étrangers sont toujours considérés comme des invités. Mais voici quelques règles essentielles pour quand vous visitez ce pays.

Les doigts: ne jamais montrer quelqu'un avec son doigt. *point*

Les têtes: ne jamais toucher la tête des enfants.

Les pieds: toujours enlever les chaussures lorsque vous entrez dans une maison, dans une mosquée ou un temple.

Les mains: toujours manger avec la main droite.

Bonjour: Il ne faut jamais serrer les mains. Il faut faire un signe de tête et un sourire. *shake*

Fill in the grid. **5**

Fingers:	you must never . . . point at people
Heads:	you must never . . touch childrens heads
Feet:	you must always . . take off your shoes . . . on entering a house, mosque or temple.
Hands:	you must always . . eat with your right hand.
Saying Hello:	you must never . . shake hands

DO NOT WRITE IN THIS MARGIN

Marks

6. There's a special article on the centre page to do with the future.

En l'an 3000. La vie de tous les jours.

Nourriture: C'est très important pour vous. Vous vous voyez manger des pilules, de la nourriture en tube ou distribuée par des machines . . . Bon appétit!

La télé aura au moins 500 chaînes. On va allumer ou éteindre la télé en claquant les mains.

Place aux robots: faire le ménage, c'est fini! Les repas, la vaisselle, le repassage etc, seront faits par des robots.

Et comment allez-vous passer votre temps?—à jouer sur vos ordinateurs ou bien à voyager dans des vaisseaux de l'espace. Génial, quoi?

(*a*) Where will you get your food from? Mention **two** things. **2**

a tube distributed from machines
or In a tablet.

(*b*) What does the article say about television? Mention **two** things. **2**

at least 500 chanells, your turn it on/off
by clapping.

(*c*) Complete the following sentences. **4**

(i) Robots will be able to help around the house by doing the ~~housework~~ ironing and the meals.

(ii) In their spare time people will play on computers or travel in spaceships.

[Turn over

DO NOT WRITE IN THIS MARGIN

Marks

7. You read an article about a dam which is being built in China.

Chine: Un barrage géant

Un gigantesque barrage est en construction en Chine. Il se trouve sur le Yang-Tsé-Kiang, un grand fleuve chinois.

Ce sera le plus grand barrage du monde. Long de 1600 mètres, haut de 183 mètres, il a été commencé en 1994. Les travaux vont continuer jusqu'en 2009. 18 000 ouvriers travaillent en ce moment à sa construction. Il s'appelle le barrage des Trois Gorges. Ce barrage servira à fabriquer 10% de l'électricité de la Chine.

What do the following numbers in the article refer to? **6**

1600	the length
183	the height
1994	the date it started
2009	the work will continue till 2009
18 000	people working on it
10%	of china's electricity is made by the dam.

Total (32)

[*END OF QUESTION PAPER*]

G

1000/407

NATIONAL QUALIFICATIONS 2000

FRIDAY, 19 MAY
11.55 AM – 12.20 PM (APPROX)

FRENCH
STANDARD GRADE
General Level
Listening Transcript

This paper must not be seen by any candidate.

The material overleaf is provided for use in an emergency only (eg the tape or equipment proving faulty) or where permission has been given in advance by SQA for the material to be read to candidates with special needs. The material must be read exactly as printed.

SCOTTISH QUALIFICATIONS AUTHORITY

Transcript—General Level

Instructions to reader(s):

For each item, read the English **once**, then read the French **three times**, with an interval of 5 seconds between the readings. On completion of the third reading, pause for the length of time indicated in brackets after each item, to allow the candidates to write their answers.

Where special arrangements have been agreed in advance to allow the reading of the material, those sections marked **(f)** should be read by a female speaker and those marked **(m)** by a male: those sections marked **(t)** should be read by the teacher.

(t) You are on holiday in France with your pen friend Antoine.

(f) or (m) **Vous êtes en vacances chez votre correspondant Antoine.**

(t) **Question number one.**

One morning Antoine's mother wakes you up.

What time is it? What are you going to do today?

(f) **Réveille-toi! Il est déjà sept heures et demie! Et c'est aujourd'hui samedi. On va rendre visite aux grands-parents!**

(*30 seconds*)

(t) **Question number two.**

She tells you what the weather will be like today.

What's today's weather forecast? Tick the correct box.

(f) **J'ai entendu la météo à la radio. Il va faire du soleil, mais un peu froid.**

(*30 seconds*)

(t) **Question number three.**

At breakfast Antoine's mother asks how you will be travelling.

How does Antoine say you will go? Why will this be handy?

(f) **—Alors, comment allez-vous faire le voyage? En autobus, ou en train?**

(m) **—Je crois qu'on va prendre l'autobus. C'est pratique parce qu'il y a un arrêt de bus juste devant la maison de mes grands-parents.**

(*30 seconds*)

(t) **Question number four.**

Antoine's mother asks him to return a couple of things to his grandfather.

What are they? Tick **two** boxes.

(f) **Ton grand-père a oublié le livre qu'il lisait et aussi ses lunettes. Tu peux les lui donner, s'il te plaît.**

(*30 seconds*)

(t) Question number five.

Antoine reminds you to take something with you.

What does he say? Fill in the gaps.

(m) **N'oublie pas ton appareil-photo. Le village de mes grands-parents est très joli, très pittoresque.**

(*30 seconds*)

(t) Question number six.

When you arrive at Antoine's grandparents' house, his grandfather welcomes you.

What two questions does he ask you? Tick **two** boxes.

(m) **Ah, bonjour! Antoine nous a beaucoup parlé de toi. C'est ta première visite en France? Combien de temps vas-tu rester ici?**

(*30 seconds*)

(t) Question number seven.

Antoine's grandmother has gone to the local shop.

What has she gone to get? Mention **two** things.

(m) **Grand-mère n'est pas ici en ce moment. Elle est allée au magasin acheter un journal et du lait.**

(*30 seconds*)

(t) Question number eight.

His grandfather continues talking.

Are the following statements true or false? Write **T** (true) or **F** (false) in the boxes below.

(m) **Elle sera de retour vers trois heures moins vingt. Elle y est allée à pied. Le magasin est au coin de la rue, à droite; c'est pas loin.**

(*30 seconds*)

(t) Question number nine.

You meet one of Antoine's friends, who is called Nathalie.

What do you learn about her? Fill in the gaps.

(f) **Je passe les vacances ici chez ma tante. En ce moment, j'aide ma tante dans son petit restaurant. Je dois mettre les tables pour le petit déjeuner et le soir, je fais la vaisselle.**

(*30 seconds*)

(t) Question number ten.

Nathalie tells you about what she is going to do.

What does she say? Fill in the gaps.

(f) **En septembre, je vais aller à l'université étudier l'informatique. Un jour, je voudrais bien travailler aux Etats-Unis.**

(*30 seconds*)

[Turn over for Questions 11, 12 and 13 on *Page four*

(t) Question number eleven.

The grandfather gives Antoine some things to take back home.

What does he give him? Mention **two** things.

(m) **Voici des choses pour ta mère: de la confiture et des légumes de notre jardin.**

(*30 seconds*)

(t) Question number twelve.

What does he then say to you? Mention **one** thing.

(m) **Mais dépêchez-vous! Sinon vous allez rater le bus!**

(*30 seconds*)

(t) Question number thirteen.

As you are leaving, Antoine reminds his grandparents about something which is happening on Tuesday.

What does he say? Mention **two** things.

(m) **N'oubliez pas que mardi, c'est l'anniversaire de mariage de Maman et Papa. Vous venez manger chez nous. D'accord?**

(*30 seconds*)

(t) End of test.

Now look over your answers.

[*END OF TRANSCRIPT*]

FOR OFFICIAL USE

G

Total Mark

1000/406

NATIONAL QUALIFICATIONS 2000

FRIDAY, 19 MAY
11.55 AM – 12.20 PM
(APPROX)

FRENCH
STANDARD GRADE
General Level
Listening

Fill in these boxes and read what is printed below.

Full name of centre

Town

Forename(s)

Surname

Date of birth
Day Month Year

Scottish candidate number

Number of seat

When you are told to do so, open your paper.

You will hear a number of short items in French. You will hear each item three times, then you will have time to write your answer.

Write your answers, **in English**, in this book, in the appropriate spaces.

You may take notes as you are listening to the French, but only in this paper.

You may **not** use a French dictionary.

You are not allowed to leave the examination room until the end of the test.

Before leaving the examination room you must give this book to the invigilator. If you do not, you may lose all the marks for this paper.

SCOTTISH QUALIFICATIONS AUTHORITY

PIB 1000/406 6/42920

DO NOT WRITE IN THIS MARGIN

Marks

You are on holiday in France with your pen friend Antoine.

Vous êtes en vacances chez votre correspondant Antoine.

1. One morning Antoine's mother wakes you up.

(*a*) What time is it? **1**

(*b*) What are you going to do today? **1**

* * * * *

2. She tells you what the weather will be like today.

What's today's weather forecast? Tick (✓) the correct box. **1**

sunny and hot		sunny and windy	
sunny and cold		windy and cold	

* * * * *

3. At breakfast Antoine's mother asks how you will be travelling.

(*a*) How does Antoine say you will go? **1**

(*b*) Why will this be handy? **1**

* * * * *

DO NOT WRITE IN THIS MARGIN

Marks

4. Antoine's mother asks him to return a couple of things to his grandfather.

What are they? Tick (✓) **two** boxes. **2**

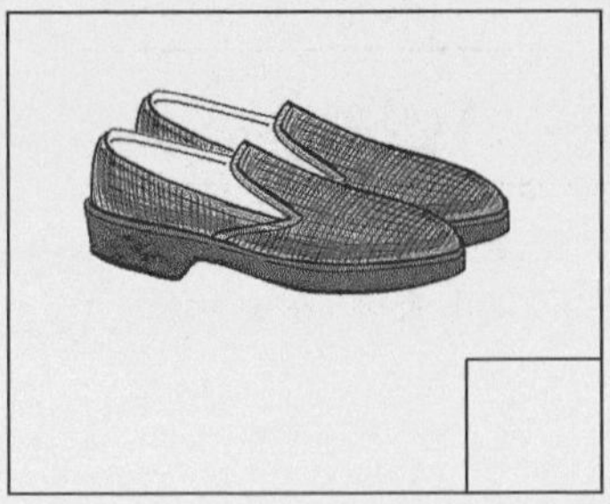

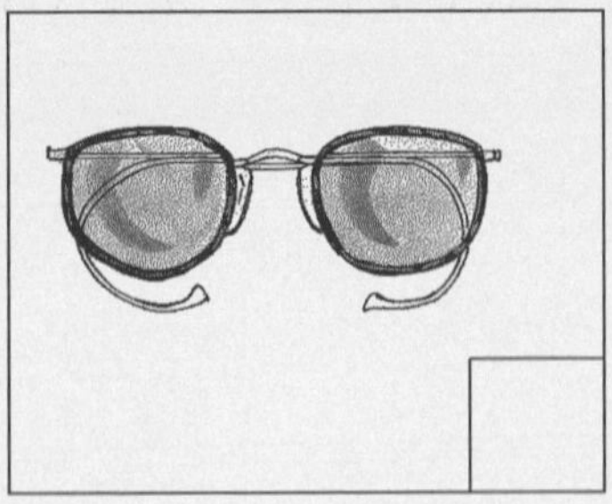

* * * * *

5. Antoine reminds you to take something with you.

What does he say? Fill in the gaps. **2**

You should take your ______________ because the village is ______________.

* * * * *

6. When you arrive at Antoine's grandparents' house, his grandfather welcomes you.

What two questions does he ask you? Tick (✓) **two** boxes. **2**

What is the weather like at home?	
Is this your first visit to France?	
How much money are you going to spend?	
How long are you going to stay?	

* * * * *

[Turn over

DO NOT WRITE IN THIS MARGIN

Marks

7. Antoine's grandmother has gone to the local shop.

What has she gone to get? Mention **two** things. **2**

____

____

* * * * *

8. His grandfather continues talking.

Are the following statements true or false? Write **T** (true) or **F** (false) in the boxes below. **3**

She will be back at 2.40.	
She has gone on her bike.	
The shop is on the left.	

* * * * *

9. You meet one of Antoine's friends, who is called Nathalie.

What do you learn about her? Fill in the gaps. **3**

Nathalie is spending her holidays ______________________.

She is helping in the restaurant. She must ______________________

for breakfast, and in the evening she ______________________.

* * * * *

10. Nathalie tells you about what she is going to do.

What does she say? Fill in the gaps. **2**

In September she is going to study ______________ at university.

One day she would like to ______________________

____.

* * * * *

DO NOT WRITE IN THIS MARGIN

Marks

11. The grandfather gives Antoine some things to take back home.

What does he give him? Mention **two** things. 2

* * * * *

12. What does he then say to you? Mention **one** thing. 1

* * * * *

13. As you are leaving, Antoine reminds his grandparents about something which is happening on Tuesday.

What does he say? Mention **two** things. 2

* * * * *

Total (26)

[*END OF QUESTION PAPER*]

[BLANK PAGE]

2001 GENERAL

FOR OFFICIAL USE

G

Total

1000/402

NATIONAL QUALIFICATIONS 2001

FRIDAY, 18 MAY
G/C 9.20 AM – 10.05 AM
F/**G** 10.05 AM – 10.50 AM

FRENCH
STANDARD GRADE
General Level
Reading

Fill in these boxes and read what is printed below.

Full name of centre

Town

Forename(s)

Surname

Date of birth
Day Month Year

Scottish candidate number

Number of seat

When you are told to do so, open your paper and write your answers **in English** in the spaces provided.

You may use a French dictionary.

Before leaving the examination room you must give this book to the invigilator. If you do not, you may lose all the marks for this paper.

SCOTTISH QUALIFICATIONS AUTHORITY ©

DO NOT WRITE IN THIS MARGIN

Marks

Your French pen friend has given you a magazine for young French readers.

1. The first article is from some young people with questions about things that interest them.

Je m'appelle Ronan et je voudrais savoir combien il y a de pays dans le monde.

Je m'appelle Anne-Sophie. Je voudrais savoir le nom du premier homme dans l'espace.

Je m'appelle Erwan. Je voudrais avoir des renseignements sur les comètes.

Je m'appelle Johanne et je voudrais savoir comment on a créé l'Univers.

Je m'appelle Marina et j'aimerais savoir qui a inventé les lunettes.

Complete the following sentences. **5**

(*a*) Ronan asks how many ______________________ in the world.

(*b*) Anne-Sophie would like to know the name of ______________________

______________________.

(*c*) Erwan would like to have ______________________.

(*d*) Johanne asks how ______________________.

(*e*) Marina wants to know who ______________________.

DO NOT WRITE IN THIS MARGIN

Marks

2. Then you spot some articles on sport. In the first one a cyclist called Jérôme talks about cycling.

"Le cyclisme, c'est ma passion.

Quand j'avais deux ans, j'ai reçu mon premier vélo, qui était rouge avec des roulettes sur les côtés. J'aimais beaucoup faire du vélo avec mon grand-père. Puis, mon grand-père est mort et j'ai arrêté le vélo. Mais plus tard, j'ai commencé à rouler avec mon père le weekend. On faisait environ trente kilomètres. Un jour, on regardait le Tour de France à la télé et j'ai décidé que je voulais faire partie d'une école de cyclisme. C'était il y a trois ans."

Which of the following statements are true? Tick (✓) **four** boxes. **4**

Jérôme started cycling two years ago.	
His first bike was red.	
His grandfather is dead now.	
He gave up cycling for a while.	
He goes roller-skating with his Dad.	
He has cycled up to 30 kilometres over a weekend.	
He cycles in the Tour de France.	

[Turn over

DO NOT WRITE IN THIS MARGIN

Marks

3. Some young people give their opinions on sport.

Le sport, c'est vital!

Moi, je faisais du tennis, mais j'ai dû arrêter car je me suis blessé au genou. Pour moi le sport, c'est fini!

Antoine, 13 ans

Avec le sport, je peux me relâcher. Faire du sport, c'est aussi faire des amis!

Eve, 12 ans

Je ne reste pas devant la télé le mercredi après-midi. Je sors pour faire de l'équitation. C'est génial!

Delphine, 12 ans

Moi, je n'aime pas trop faire du sport au collège. Par contre, je pratique le tennis de table au club des jeunes. Et là, j'adore ça!

Claire, 14 ans

Le sport c'est bien, mais il y a d'autres choses dans la vie. Mon conseil aux fanatiques de sport: intéressez-vous à tout!

Arthur, 14 ans

Moi, je ne suis pas sportif, mais j'aime regarder le sport à la télé.

Pierre, 17 ans

Who made the following statements? Put the correct name in each box. **4**

I stopped doing sport because of injury.	
There's more to life than sport!	
Sport is for relaxing and making friends.	
Sport gets me out of the house.	

DO NOT WRITE IN THIS MARGIN

Marks

4. You read about an accident involving a young boy.

Accident de voiture

En Charente, un garçon de quatorze ans a volé la voiture de sa mère. Après quelques minutes, il a perdu contrôle et a renversé la voiture. Résultat: des fractures au bras et à la jambe, et deux semaines à l'hôpital.

(*a*) What did the boy steal? 1

____

(*b*) Say what happened next. Mention any **three** things. 3

____

____

____

[Turn over

DO NOT WRITE IN THIS MARGIN

Marks

5. Then you read something about the Internet.

L'internet, c'est vraiment génial!

L'internet, à mon avis, c'est génial et très pratique. On peut surfer et jouer avec des copains. En plus, on peut envoyer des messages presqu'immédiatement. Le Ministre de l'Education a lancé un grand plan dans tous les établissements scolaires parce qu'il trouve que l'Internet n'est pas assez utilisé dans les écoles. Il promet que chaque étudiant aura son adresse électronique en l'an 2002. Chic!

(*a*) Apart from "surfing the net", what else can you use the Internet for? **2**

___

___

(*b*) Why has the Minister of Education launched his new campaign in schools? **1**

___

(*c*) What promise does he make for the year 2002? **1**

___

Marks

6. The magazine has an item about Afghanistan today.

Afghanistan aujourd'hui!

Il y a deux ans, en Afghanistan, on a interdit aux femmes de sortir sans voiles; on a interdit aux hommes de se raser la barbe, et aussi, les enfants n'ont pas le droit d'écouter la musique qu'ils aiment. Puis, en plus, on a demandé aux Afghans de jeter leurs postes de télé. Pourquoi? Le gouvernement pense que les bulletins d'informations du monde extérieur sont "dangereux".

Are these statements true or false? Write T (True) or F (False) in the boxes below. **4**

Women have to wear a veil when they go out.	
Men have to shave off their beards.	
Children are allowed to listen to all kinds of music.	
The Afghans have been asked to get rid of their televisions.	

[Turn over

DO NOT WRITE IN THIS MARGIN

Marks

7. Some young people have been helping clean up the countryside.

Nettoyage de printemps

Samedi 24 et dimanche 25 mars, c'était la grande opération de "nettoyage de printemps". Il y avait du travail: nettoyer les berges des rivières, les bords de plages, les bois.

Which areas have they cleaned? Tick (✓) **three** boxes. **3**

streets	
woods	
riverbanks	
parks	
beaches	
pavements	

DO NOT WRITE IN THIS MARGIN

Marks

8. At the end of the magazine you see an article about teachers.

Un prof génial? Mais, oui, ça existe!

C'est quoi, un prof génial? Emilie nous parle:

"La différence entre un prof 'bof-bof' et un prof 'top-top', c'est son intérêt pour ses élèves. Par exemple, ma prof d'espagnol est géniale. Elle est très sévère et elle nous donne beaucoup de devoirs. Il y a des élèves qui ont parfois des difficultés, mais la prof les aide beaucoup. Ils travaillent plus dur, et reçoivent de bonnes notes. On a l'impression qu'elle aime sa matière, et elle sait bien nous intéresser."

What does Emilie think makes a good teacher? Mention any **four** things. **4**

Total (32)

[*END OF QUESTION PAPER*]

[BLANK PAGE]

G

1000/407

NATIONAL QUALIFICATIONS 2001

FRIDAY, 18 MAY
11.55 AM – 12.20 PM
(APPROX)

FRENCH
STANDARD GRADE
General Level
Listening Transcript

This paper must not be seen by any candidate.

The material overleaf is provided for use in an emergency only (eg the tape or equipment proving faulty) or where permission has been given in advance by SQA for the material to be read to candidates with special needs. The material must be read exactly as printed.

Transcript—General Level

Instructions to reader(s):

For each item, read the English **once**, then read the French **three times**, with an interval of 5 seconds between the readings. On completion of the third reading, pause for the length of time indicated in brackets after each item, to allow the candidates to write their answers.

Where special arrangements have been agreed in advance to allow the reading of the material, those sections marked **(f)** should be read by a female speaker and those marked **(m)** by a male: those sections marked **(t)** should be read by the teacher.

(t) You are staying with your pen friend, Jeanne.

Tu loges chez ta correspondante, Jeanne.

(t) Question number one.

One day you go shopping with her. In town she sees one of her teachers.

Which subject does he teach?

What does she say about him? Mention any **two** things.

(f) **Tiens, tu vois cet homme-là? C'est mon prof d'histoire. C'est mon prof préféré. Je l'aime bien. Il s'intéresse beaucoup à ses élèves.**

(*30 seconds*)

(t) Question number two.

She tells you what sports they do at school.

In which season do they do each sport? Complete the grid.

(f) **A mon collège, on fait beaucoup de sports. Ça dépend un peu de la saison. On fait du tennis dehors au printemps. On joue au volley dans le gymnase en hiver.**

(*30 seconds*)

(t) Question number three.

Jeanne goes into a shop to buy something she needs for school.

What is she looking for? Tick the correct box.

How much can she spend? Tick the correct box.

(f) or (m) **—Bonjour, vous désirez?**

(f) **—Bonjour Madame. Je cherche des chaussures de tennis, mais pas trop chères. Je n'ai que cinq cents francs à dépenser.**

(*30 seconds*)

(t) **Question number four.**

You go to a café. In the café she asks you to do something.

What does she want you to do?

Why?

(f) **Tu peux commander les boissons? Comme ça tu pourras pratiquer ton français!**

(*30 seconds*)

(t) **Question number five.**

Then you go into the tourist information centre.

What two questions does Jeanne ask the assistant? Tick **two** boxes.

(f) **Demain, on va à la campagne visiter le vieux château qui se trouve à dix kilomètres d'ici. S'il vous plaît, combien coûte l'entrée au château? Et à quelle heure part le bus pour y aller?**

(*30 seconds*)

(t) **Question number six.**

When you get home, Jeanne tells you about her aunt who is coming to visit this afternoon.

Why does she hope her uncle will come as well?

(f) **Ma tante Annette va nous rendre visite cet après-midi. J'espère que mon oncle Marc va l'accompagner. Il est très sympa.**

(*30 seconds*)

(t) **Question number seven.**

She tells you about her uncle.

Tick the correct box to say if each statement is True or False.

(f) **Mon oncle Marc a une vie très intéressante. Il écrit des articles sur la nature pour les magazines. Chaque année, il passe trois ou quatre mois dans un pays différent. Il étudie les animaux du pays, mais sa passion, c'est les fleurs et les plantes.**

(*30 seconds*)

(t) **Question number eight.**

When her uncle arrives he talks about his latest trip.

Complete the following sentences.

(m) **L'année dernière, je suis allé en Amérique du Sud. J'ai passé onze semaines dans la jungle. J'ai pris des centaines de photos et j'ai fait des interviews avec des habitants de la région.**

(*30 seconds*)

(t) **Question number nine.**

What difficulties did he have on this trip? Mention any **two** things.

(m) **Quand j'étais dans la jungle, il faisait trop chaud, donc je suis tombé malade. J'avais mal au ventre et j'avais de la fièvre.**

(*30 seconds*)

[Turn over for Questions 10 and 11 on *Page four*

(t) Question number ten.

Now that he is home, his routine is very different.

How are the next few weeks planned? Fill in the timetable. Write **one** thing for each week.

(m) **La première semaine, je vais me relaxer car je suis très fatigué. Puis la deuxième semaine, je vais développer toutes mes photos. La troisième semaine, on m'a demandé de parler de mon voyage dans une émission de radio.**

(*30 seconds*)

(t) Question number eleven.

Before the visitors leave, Jeanne's uncle makes a suggestion.

What does he say? Mention any **one** thing.

(m) **Bon alors, est-ce que vous voulez nous rendre visite samedi prochain? Je vais préparer un repas spécial!**

(*30 seconds*)

(t) End of test.

Now look over your answers.

[*END OF TRANSCRIPT*]

FOR OFFICIAL USE

G

Total Mark

1000/406

NATIONAL QUALIFICATIONS 2001

FRIDAY, 18 MAY
11.55 AM – 12.20 PM
(APPROX)

FRENCH
STANDARD GRADE
General Level
Listening

Fill in these boxes and read what is printed below.

Full name of centre

Town

Forename(s)

Surname

Date of birth
Day Month Year

Scottish candidate number

Number of seat

When you are told to do so, open your paper.

You will hear a number of short items in French. You will hear each item three times, then you will have time to write your answer.

Write your answers, **in English**, in this book, in the appropriate spaces.

You may take notes as you are listening to the French, but only in this paper.

You may **not** use a French dictionary.

You are not allowed to leave the examination room until the end of the test.

Before leaving the examination room you must give this book to the invigilator. If you do not, you may lose all the marks for this paper.

SCOTTISH QUALIFICATIONS AUTHORITY

PIB 1000/406 6/3/45720

Marks

You are staying with your pen friend, Jeanne.

Tu loges chez ta correspondante, Jeanne.

1. One day you go shopping with her. In town she sees one of her teachers.

(*a*) Which subject does he teach? **1**

____

(*b*) What does she say about him? Mention any **two** things. **2**

____

____

* * * * *

2. She tells you what sports they do at school.

In which season do they do each sport? Complete the grid. **2**

seasons		

* * * * *

DO NOT WRITE IN THIS MARGIN

Marks

3. Jeanne goes into a shop to buy something she needs for school.

(*a*) What is she looking for? Tick (✓) the correct box. **1**

(*b*) How much can she spend? Tick (✓) the correct box. **1**

550 francs	
50 francs	
500 francs	

* * * * *

4. You go to a café. In the café she asks you to do something.

(*a*) What does she want you to do? **1**

____

(*b*) Why? **1**

____

* * * * *

[Turn over

DO NOT WRITE IN THIS MARGIN

Marks

5. Then you go into the tourist information centre.

What two questions does Jeanne ask the assistant?

Tick (✓) **two** boxes. 2

What is there to see at the château?	
What time does the bus leave?	
How much does it cost to get into the château?	
Can we buy champagne there?	

* * * * *

6. When you get home, Jeanne tells you about her aunt who is coming to visit this afternoon.

Why does she hope her uncle will come as well? 1

____

* * * * *

7. She tells you about her uncle.

Tick (✓) the correct box to say if each statement is True or False. 4

	True	**False**
Her uncle is a writer.		
He visits a different country every year.		
He spends only 3–4 months of the year in France.		
He is particularly interested in plants.		

* * * * *

DO NOT WRITE IN THIS MARGIN

Marks

8. When her uncle arrives he talks about his latest trip.

Complete the following sentences.

(*a*) Her uncle went to ______________________________. **1**

(*b*) He stayed there for ______________________________. **1**

(*c*) On his trip he ______________________________ **1**

and ______________________________. **1**

* * * * *

9. What difficulties did he have on this trip? Mention any **two** things. **2**

____

____

* * * * *

10. Now that he is home, his routine is very different.

How are the next few weeks planned? Fill in the timetable. Write **one** thing for each week. **3**

Week 1	
Week 2	
Week 3	

* * * * *

11. Before the visitors leave, Jeanne's uncle makes a suggestion.

What does he say? Mention any **one** thing. **1**

____

* * * * *

Total (26)

[*END OF QUESTION PAPER*]

[BLANK PAGE]

2002 GENERAL

FOR OFFICIAL USE

G

Total

1000/402

NATIONAL QUALIFICATIONS 2002

WEDNESDAY, 15 MAY
10.05 AM–10.50 AM

FRENCH
STANDARD GRADE
General Level
Reading

Fill in these boxes and read what is printed below.

Full name of centre

Town

Forename(s)

Surname

Date of birth
Day Month Year

Scottish candidate number

Number of seat

When you are told to do so, open your paper and write your answers **in English** in the spaces provided.

You may use a French dictionary.

Before leaving the examination room you must give this book to the invigilator. If you do not, you may lose all the marks for this paper.

SCOTTISH QUALIFICATIONS AUTHORITY

DO NOT WRITE IN THIS MARGIN

Marks

1. You read about a record held by a young English girl.

Une jeune Anglaise de douze ans a traversé la Manche à la nage. C'est la fille la plus jeune à avoir fait cette traversée.
Bravo pour ce nouveau record!

(*a*) How did she get across the English channel? **1**

(*b*) What record does she hold? **1**

2. You come across an advert for a helpline for young people.

Fil santé jeunes.

Fais le 08 00 23 52 36

- C'est un numéro gratuit et anonyme
- La ligne est ouverte entre huit heures du matin et minuit
- C'est pour tes questions—rapports avec les parents, amour, santé . . .

(*a*) What are you told about this helpline number? Mention any **one** thing. **1**

(*b*) Between which times could you phone? **1**

(*c*) What would you use this helpline for? Mention any **one** thing. **1**

DO NOT WRITE IN THIS MARGIN

Marks

3. Below are some details about an international agreement to protect children's rights, which France signed.

A — L'enseignement primaire et secondaire doit être gratuit.

B — L'enfant a droit au repos, aux jeux et activités récréatives de son âge.

C — L'enfant a *le droit d'exprimer son opinion (sauf si ce sont des insultes).

D — L'enfant ne doit pas souffrir de discriminations à cause des origines de ses parents.

E — L'enfant doit être protégé contre toute violence, abandon, ou négligence.

F — L'enfant ne doit pas être séparé de ses parents.

* le droit = the right

Match each of the following headings with one of the statements above. Put the correct letter in each box. **4**

Children have . . .

the right not to be abused.	
the right to education.	
the right to leisure.	
the right to express their views.	

[Turn over

DO NOT WRITE IN THIS MARGIN

Marks

4. The international agreement also covers children's rights where parents are divorced.

> En cas de divorce, l'enfant peut choisir le parent avec qui il voudrait vivre. Il a le droit d'être écouté par le juge.

According to the agreement, what rights does the child have? Mention **two** things. **2**

____

____

____

5. You then read about Alexander Selkirk, a Scottish explorer.

> Alexander est né en 1676. A 19 ans, il s'embarque comme matelot. Cette expérience finit mal—il est capturé par des pirates français et il reste leur prisonnier pendant deux ans. Après deux ans, il continue son aventure sur un bateau anglais. Mais il se dispute avec le capitaine et il débarque sur une île déserte.

Which of these statements are true? Tick (✓) **three** boxes. **3**

He set off on his travels in 1676.	
He was a sailor for 19 years.	
French pirates captured him.	
He was a prisoner for 2 years.	
He became captain of a ship.	
He ended up on a desert island.	

DO NOT WRITE IN THIS MARGIN

Marks

6. The story continues.

Pas de problème pour la nourriture parce qu' il y avait beaucoup de chèvres sur l'île. Pour compter les jours, il fait une coche sur un arbre chaque matin avec un canif. Après quatre ans, un autre bateau arrive. L'histoire d'Alexander a inspiré à Daniel Defoe son célèbre roman *Robinson Crusoé*.

(*a*) What was his main source of food? **1**

____

(*b*) How did he keep track of time? **1**

____

____

[Turn over

DO NOT WRITE IN THIS MARGIN

Marks

7. After the story there are some handy hints for would-be castaways, who want to put up a tent.

A Vérifie que le terrain n'est pas en pente.	B Evite les endroits sales où il y a beaucoup d'ordures.
C Ne place pas l'ouverture de la tente face au vent.	D Ne plante pas la tente près des arbres isolés en cas d'orage.

Match the hints above to **four** of the pictures below. Put the correct letters in four of the boxes. **4**

1

2

3

4

5

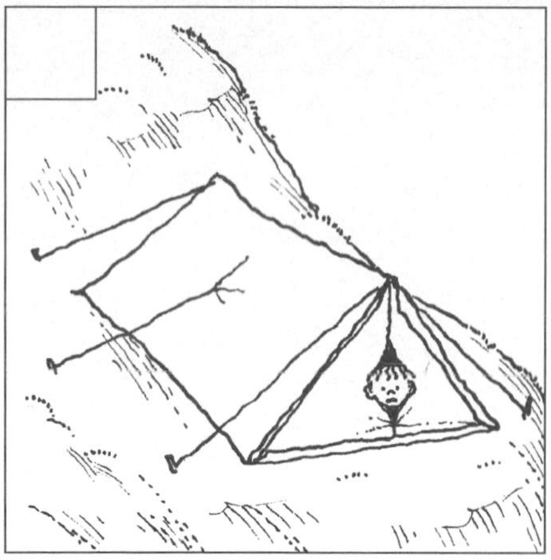

6

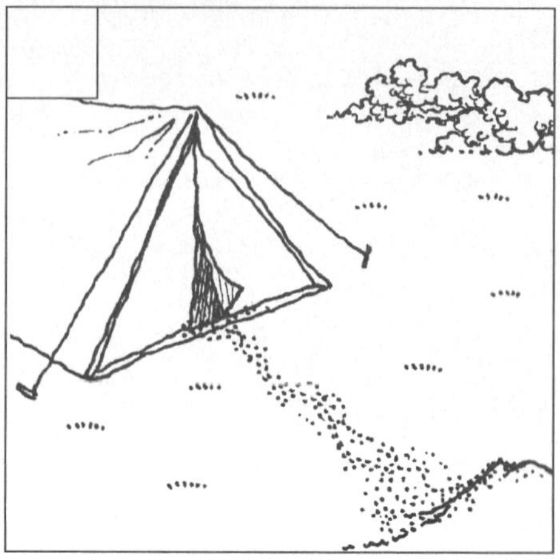

DO NOT WRITE IN THIS MARGIN

Marks

8. You are given advice on how to light a campfire safely.

* ne fais jamais de feu en forêt
* n'abandonne jamais un feu
* choisis un endroit loin de la tente
* demande toujours l'autorisation
* garde toujours de l'eau pour éteindre le feu

What are you told? Mention any **three** things. 3

[Turn over

DO NOT WRITE IN THIS MARGIN

Marks

9. You read an article about a very old lady.

Ana Molina vient de réaliser le rêve de sa vie. A l'âge de 102 ans, elle a fini d'écrire un livre sur son enfance et sur la vie au début du vingtième siècle.

Après la mort de son père, elle avait dû quitter l'école à l'âge de douze ans. Pourquoi? Elle était responsable de ses huit frères et soeurs, donc elle a dû rester à la maison pour s'occuper d'eux.

(*a*) Ana Molina has just achieved her life's ambition of writing a book. What was it about? Mention **two** things. **2**

(*b*) What event caused her to leave school when she was 12 years old? **1**

(*c*) Why did she have to leave school then? **1**

DO NOT WRITE IN THIS MARGIN

Marks

10. In a survey of young people's views on adoption, the following answers were given.

Grâce à l'adoption, un enfant peut trouver une famille. Mais, s'il a des frères et des soeurs, on ne doit pas les séparer.
Régis

Nous avons adopté un petit frère. Maintenant, on a moins de tranquillité. Mais on rigole plus souvent.
Marie

C'est très bien d'adopter un enfant, et pour les parents et pour les enfants, mais les étapes qu'il faut surmonter sont difficiles.
Paul

Moi, si j'étais adoptée, j'aimerais le savoir.
Lola

Je suis adoptée à l'étranger. Je suis arrivée en France avec mes parents adoptifs un 25 décembre.
Mélanie

Maman est tombée gravement malade. A l'hôpital, nous sommes devenus amis avec le médecin. Il m'a adopté quand maman est morte.
Louis

Aujourd'hui, je vis très bien mon adoption, à part les insultes racistes et les questions embarrassantes.
Anne

Who makes each of the following comments? Write **one** name after each comment. **5**

I was adopted abroad. ______________

Life is noisier but happier since our family adopted a child. ______________

Brothers and sisters shouldn't be split up by adoption. ______________

I was adopted by my Mum's doctor. ______________

I would want to know if I was adopted. ______________

Total (32)

[END OF QUESTION PAPER]

[BLANK PAGE]

G

1000/407

NATIONAL QUALIFICATIONS 2002

WEDNESDAY, 15 MAY
1.45 PM – 2.10 PM
(APPROX)

FRENCH
STANDARD GRADE
General Level
Listening Transcript

This paper must not be seen by any candidate.

The material overleaf is provided for use in an emergency only (eg the tape or equipment proving faulty) or where permission has been given in advance by SQA for the material to be read to candidates with special needs. The material must be read exactly as printed.

SCOTTISH QUALIFICATIONS AUTHORITY

Transcript—General Level

Instructions to reader(s):

For each item, read the English **once**, then read the French **three times**, with an interval of 5 seconds between the readings. On completion of the third reading, pause for the length of time indicated in brackets after each item, to allow the candidates to write their answers.

Where special arrangements have been agreed in advance to allow the reading of the material, those sections marked **(f)** should be read by a female speaker and those marked **(m)** by a male: those sections marked **(t)** should be read by the teacher.

(t) You are staying with your French pen friend, Maurice.

(m) or (f) Vous logez chez votre correspondant français, Maurice.

(t) Question number one.

You are going to visit his school today.

How are you going to get there?

(m) **D'habitude je prends le bus, mais aujourd'hui Papa nous emmène en voiture.**

(*30 seconds*)

(t) Question number two.

When do lessons start in Maurice's school? Tick the correct box.

(m) **Il faut quitter la maison vers huit heures, car les cours commencent à huit heures et demie.**

(*30 seconds*)

(t) Question number three.

Maurice tells you about the subjects he does at school.

What does he say about maths? Tick **two** boxes.

What does he tell you about the geography teacher? Tick **two** boxes.

(m) **Les maths, c'est ma matière préférée; c'est très intéressant et utile, mais la géo, c'est autre chose! Je n'aime pas ça! Le prof est très sympa, mais il nous donne trop de devoirs.**

(*30 seconds*)

(t) Question number four.

You ask him what usually happens at lunchtime.

What does he tell you? Complete the sentences.

(m) **L'heure du déjeuner est de midi à deux heures. C'est normal en France. Beaucoup d'élèves mangent à la cantine, car ils habitent trop loin du collège pour rentrer à la maison.**

(*30 seconds*)

(t) **Question number five.**

What else does Maurice say? Tick **two** boxes.

(m) **Les repas sont très bons, mais ce que je n'aime pas, c'est que à la cantine, il y a toujours beaucoup de bruit. Ce n'est pas du tout relaxant! Je préfère manger dans une atmosphère calme.**

(*30 seconds*)

(t) **Question number six.**

You ask Maurice what he and his friends usually do after lunch.

What does he say? Tick **two** boxes.

(m) **D'habitude on bavarde avec les copains, mais quelquefois on joue au tennis de table au foyer. J'aime ça!**

(*30 seconds*)

(t) **Question number seven.**

Maurice's mother tells you about a visit she made to Scotland.

When did she visit Scotland?

Why did she like staying in Youth Hostels?

(f) **J'ai visité l'Ecosse avec deux copains quand j'avais dix-neuf ans. On a logé dans des auberges de jeunesse; c'était bien parce que j'ai fait la connaissance de beaucoup de jeunes de toutes nationalités.**

(*30 seconds*)

(t) **Question number eight.**

She goes on to tell you what she thought about Scotland.

Mention any **one** thing she liked about Scotland.

Mention any **one** thing she disliked.

(f) **Ce qui m'a beaucoup impressionnée, c'était les montagnes. Et aussi, les gens étaient tous très sympa. Mais il faut dire que je n'aimais pas tellement le climat. J'avais toujours froid!**

(*30 seconds*)

(t) **Question number nine.**

Maurice's mother talks about the evening meal.

What does she say will be on the menu? Tick **three** boxes.

(f) **Demain je ne travaille pas, donc je vais préparer quelque chose de spécial. D'abord, une bouillabaisse,—ça, c'est une soupe de poissons—puis, comme plat principal, du poulet rôti avec une bonne sauce, et pour le dessert, une mousse au chocolat.**

(*30 seconds*)

[Turn over for Questions 10 to 14 on *Page four*

(t) Question number ten.

She has also been thinking about an outing for you and Maurice tomorrow evening.

What does she suggest?

Why does she think you might be interested? Mention any **one** thing.

(f) **Demain soir il y a un match de basket au centre sportif. Ton cousin va jouer pour notre ville et nous avons des billets gratuits. Vous pouvez y aller, si vous voulez.**

(30 seconds)

(t) Question number eleven.

What does Maurice think about this idea? Mention any **one** thing.

He has another idea. What is it? Mention any **one** thing.

(m) **Oh, Maman! Je ne veux pas! C'est ennuyeux! En plus, je veux aller au club des jeunes demain soir pour rencontrer mes copains.**

(30 seconds)

(t) Question number twelve.

Maurice's mother mentions that it will be hard for you to get home.

What is the problem? Mention **one** thing.

(f) **Le vendredi soir après dix heures il n'y a plus de bus pour rentrer.**

(30 seconds)

(t) Question number thirteen.

Maurice suggests a way round the problem. What does he suggest?

(m) **Mais Papa pourrait venir nous chercher en voiture.**

(30 seconds)

(t) Question number fourteen.

Maurice's mother says that this would not work. Why not?

(f) **Ah, non, Maurice. Pas possible. Ton père doit partir pour l'Angleterre demain et il va y passer deux jours.**

(30 seconds)

(t) End of test.

Now look over your answers.

[*END OF TRANSCRIPT*]

FOR OFFICIAL USE

G

Total Mark

1000/406

NATIONAL QUALIFICATIONS 2002

WEDNESDAY, 15 MAY
1.45 PM – 2.10 PM
(APPROX)

FRENCH
STANDARD GRADE
General Level
Listening

Fill in these boxes and read what is printed below.

Full name of centre

Town

Forename(s)

Surname

Date of birth
Day Month Year

Scottish candidate number

Number of seat

When you are told to do so, open your paper.

You will hear a number of short items in French. You will hear each item three times, then you will have time to write your answer.

Write your answers, **in English**, in this book, in the appropriate spaces.

You may take notes as you are listening to the French, but only in this paper.

You may **not** use a French dictionary.

You are not allowed to leave the examination room until the end of the test.

Before leaving the examination room you must give this book to the invigilator. If you do not, you may lose all the marks for this paper.

Scottish Qualifications Authority

PIB 1000/406 6/45870

DO NOT WRITE IN THIS MARGIN

Marks

You are staying with your French pen friend, Maurice.

Vous logez chez votre correspondant français, Maurice.

1. You are going to visit his school today.

How are you going to get there? **1**

____

* * * * *

2. When do lessons start in Maurice's school? Tick (✓) the correct box. **1**

8.00		8.20		8.30	

* * * * *

3. Maurice tells you about the subjects he does at school.

(*a*) What does he say about maths? Tick (✓) **two** boxes. **2**

He likes the teacher.	
It's interesting.	
It's easy.	
It's useful.	

(*b*) What does he tell you about the geography teacher? Tick (✓) **two** boxes. **2**

He doesn't like him.	
He's nice.	
He doesn't give homework.	
He gives too much homework.	

* * * * *

DO NOT WRITE IN THIS MARGIN

Marks

4. You ask him what usually happens at lunchtime.

What does he tell you? Complete the sentences. **2**

Lunchtime is between ______________________________ .

Many pupils eat in the canteen because they ____________________

____ .

* * * * *

5. What else does Maurice say? Tick (✓) **two** boxes. **2**

The meals are good.	
The meals are expensive.	
The canteen is never quiet.	
He finds the canteen relaxing.	

* * * * *

6. You ask Maurice what he and his friends usually do after lunch.

What does he say? Tick (✓) **two** boxes. **2**

* * * * *

[Turn over

DO NOT WRITE IN THIS MARGIN

Marks

7. Maurice's mother tells you about a visit she made to Scotland.

(*a*) When did she visit Scotland? **1**

____

(*b*) Why did she like staying in Youth Hostels? **1**

____

* * * * *

8. She goes on to tell you what she thought about Scotland.

(*a*) Mention any **one** thing she liked about Scotland. **1**

____

(*b*) Mention any **one** thing she disliked. **1**

____

* * * * *

9. Maurice's mother talks about the evening meal.

What does she say will be on the menu? Tick (✓) **three** boxes. **3**

Starter	fish		fish soup	
Main course	chicken		steak	
Dessert	chocolate cake		chocolate mousse	

* * * * *

10. She has also been thinking about an outing for you and Maurice tomorrow evening.

(*a*) What does she suggest? **1**

____

(*b*) Why does she think you might be interested? Mention any **one** thing. **1**

____

* * * * *

Marks | DO NOT WRITE IN THIS MARGIN

11. (*a*) What does Maurice think about this idea? Mention any **one** thing. **1**

(*b*) He has another idea. What is it? Mention any **one** thing. **1**

* * * * *

12. Maurice's mother mentions that it will be hard for you to get home.

What is the problem? Mention **one** thing. **1**

* * * * *

13. Maurice suggests a way round the problem. What does he suggest? **1**

* * * * *

14. Maurice's mother says that this would not work. Why not? **1**

* * * * *

Total (26)

[*END OF QUESTION PAPER*]

[BLANK PAGE]

2003 GENERAL

FOR OFFICIAL USE

G

Total

1000/402

NATIONAL QUALIFICATIONS 2003

WEDNESDAY, 14 MAY
10.05 AM–10.50 AM

FRENCH
STANDARD GRADE
General Level
Reading

Fill in these boxes and read what is printed below.

Full name of centre

Town

Forename(s)

Surname

Date of birth
Day Month Year

Scottish candidate number

Number of seat

When you are told to do so, open your paper and write your answers **in English** in the spaces provided.

You may use a French dictionary.

Before leaving the examination room you must give this book to the invigilator. If you do not, you may lose all the marks for this paper.

SCOTTISH QUALIFICATIONS AUTHORITY

THB 1000/402 6/45670

DO NOT WRITE IN THIS MARGIN

Marks

1. You see this article about the singer, Céline Dion.

Céline Dion est née le 30 mars 1968 à Charlemagne au Québec, région francophone du Canada. C'est la plus jeune d'une famille de quatorze enfants.

A l'âge de douze ans, la jeune Céline enregistre sa première chanson dans la cuisine familiale. C'est sa mère qui l'a écrite pour elle! Le premier album, «La Voix du Bon Dieu», paraît en 1981 et est Disque d'Or en 1982. Céline a quatorze ans.

Complete these sentences: **3**

Céline is the ________________ of fourteen children.

Her first song was recorded in the ________________ of her home.

She had her first gold disc when she was ________________ years old.

2. The article continues.

C'est en 1999 que Céline connaît son plus grand succès avec la chanson «My Heart Will Go On», le thème principal du film «Titanic». A la fin de la même année, elle est fêtée par sa compagnie de disques, Sony, pour avoir vendu cent millions d'albums.

Le premier janvier 2000, Céline quitte la scène pour avoir un enfant. Son fils, René-Charles, est né le 25 janvier 2001.

Complete these sentences: **2**

"My Heart Will Go On" was her ________________ success.

She gave up singing in 2000 in order to ________________ .

DO NOT WRITE IN THIS MARGIN

Marks

3. You read about an exciting scientific discovery.

Une planète géante a été découverte par les astronomes qui travaillent dans un observatoire situé au Chili, à quatre cents kilomètres au nord de la capitale. La planète se trouve en dehors du système solaire à une distance de cinquante-six années-lumière de la Terre.

Are these statements True or False? Write **T** (True) or **F** (False) in each box. **3**

A very large planet has been discovered. ☐

It was discovered by astronomers working in the capital of Chile. ☐

It is 56 light years from Earth. ☐

4. You read this article about children who are victims of war.

Les enfants victimes de la guerre

- Des enfants sont actuellement engagés dans des guerres dans plus de quarante pays.
- Plus de trois cent mille sont âgés de moins de treize ans.
- Plus de deux millions d'enfants sur notre planète sont morts à cause de la guerre.
- Sur les treize millions de réfugiés dans le monde, la moitié sont des enfants.

Complete these sentences: **4**

Today, children are involved in war in more than ____________________.

More than 300 000 of these children are ____________________.

More than 2 million children on our planet ____________________.

Out of the 13 million refugees in the world, ______________ are children.

[Turn over

DO NOT WRITE IN THIS MARGIN

Marks

5. You find an article about looking after dogs.

Comment élever votre chien.

Vous avez décidé d'adopter un chien? Eh bien, c'est une décision très importante; avoir un animal, ça donne beaucoup de responsabilités. Il faut demander conseil aux professionnels qui s'occupent des chiens.

(*a*) You should think carefully before getting a dog. Why? **1**

____

____

(*b*) Who should you approach for advice? **1**

____

____

6. The article goes on to give some tips on looking after your dog.

- Il faut le promener tous les jours.
- Il faut lui donner de la nourriture saine.
- Il faut l'emmener régulièrement chez le vétérinaire.
- Il ne faut jamais le laisser dans la voiture quand il fait chaud.

Complete the following sentences: **4**

To look after your dog properly,

you must ______________________________ every day.

you must give him ______________________________ .

you must take him ______________________________ .

you must never leave him ______________________________ .

DO NOT WRITE IN THIS MARGIN

Marks

7. You read this article about a young author.

Mon premier livre

Je m'appelle Patrick Delatour, j'ai seize ans et j'habite à Antibes qui se trouve sur la Côte d'Azur entre Nice et Cannes. J'adore lire et écrire, et j'ai récemment écrit mon premier livre qui s'appelle "Une Vie Simple".

Mon livre parle de Marcel, un jeune homme qui passe de l'adolescence à l'âge adulte.

D'abord, il rencontre Antoinette, une jeune fille très jolie, et il tombe amoureux d'elle. Mais hélas, le père d'Antoinette trouve un emploi à Lyon et la famille déménage. Les jeunes gens sont séparés et Marcel est très triste.

(*a*) What are Patrick's main hobbies? **2**

____

____

(*b*) What makes this book so special for Patrick? **1**

____

(*c*) What is "Une Vie Simple" about? **1**

____

(*d*) In the book, Marcel falls in love with Antoinette. Why do they become separated? **1**

____

[Turn over

DO NOT WRITE IN THIS MARGIN

Marks

8. The article about Patrick's book goes on.

> Puis, il y a des difficultés dans le mariage des parents de Marcel. Enfin, ils décident de divorcer. Pour Marcel, il y a un choix difficile. Il va habiter chez sa mère ou son père?
>
> Le personnage principal de mon livre s'appelle Marcel, mais, vous l'avez bien deviné . . . oui . . . c'est moi!

(*a*) When Marcel's parents get divorced, what decision does he have to make? **1**

____

(*b*) What surprising information are we given at the end of the article? **1**

____

DO NOT WRITE IN THIS MARGIN

Marks

9. You read this article about Fabienne Dumoulin, a journalist on a local newspaper in France.

Je suis journaliste

NOM : Dumoulin

PRÉNOM : Fabienne

ÂGE : 26 ans

ÉDUCATION : Diplôme d'anglais; deux ans à une école de journalisme.

PROFESSION : Journaliste

Il est neuf heures du matin. Fabienne arrive au bureau. Elle explique:

"Le matin, il ne se passe pas grand-chose; d'abord, je lis les journaux et mon courrier. J'appelle la police et les pompiers pour voir s'il y a eu des incidents dans la ville pendant la nuit. Quelquefois, je travaille sur les articles que je n'ai pas finis."

(*a*) What does Fabienne do when she arrives at the office? Mention **one** thing. **1**

(*b*) Why does she telephone the police and the fire brigade? **1**

(*c*) What else does she do in the mornings? **1**

[Turn over for Question 10 on *Page eight*

DO NOT WRITE IN THIS MARGIN

Marks

10. Fabienne continues her story.

"L'après-midi, je ne suis pas au bureau. Je vais à une réunion, ou je vais dans les rues pour parler aux gens. A ce moment-là, je prends toutes les photos moi-même. J'entre en contact avec toutes sortes de gens, et ça, c'est intéressant."

"A la fin de l'après-midi, je rentre au bureau et je travaille sur mon ordinateur. En général, je finis vers six heures, mais quelquefois je dois travailler le soir à la maison."

(*a*) Mention any **two** things she does in the afternoons. **2**

____

____

(*b*) What does she find interesting about her job? **1**

____

(*c*) What does she sometimes have to do in the evenings? **1**

____

Total (32)

[*END OF QUESTION PAPER*]

G

1000/407

NATIONAL QUALIFICATIONS 2003

WEDNESDAY, 14 MAY
1.45 PM – 2.10 PM (APPROX)

FRENCH STANDARD GRADE

General Level
Listening Transcript

This paper must not be seen by any candidate.

The material overleaf is provided for use in an emergency only (eg the CD or equipment proving faulty) or where permission has been given in advance by SQA for the material to be read to candidates with special needs. The material must be read exactly as printed.

SCOTTISH QUALIFICATIONS AUTHORITY

Transcript—General Level

Instructions to reader(s):

For each item, read the English **once**, then read the French **three times**, with an interval of 5 seconds between the readings. On completion of the third reading, pause for the length of time indicated in brackets after each item, to allow the candidates to write their answers.

Where special arrangements have been agreed in advance to allow the reading of the material, those sections marked **(f)** should be read by a female speaker and those marked **(m)** by a male: those sections marked **(t)** should be read by the teacher.

(t) You are on holiday in France. You are spending a fortnight with your French pen-friend, Marie.

(m) or (f) **Vous êtes en vacances en France. Vous passez une quinzaine chez votre correspondante française, Marie.**

(t) **Question number one.**

Marie talks to you about pocket money.

When does Marie get her pocket money? Who does she get her pocket money from?

(f) **Moi, je reçois mon argent de poche le vendredi soir. Mon père me le donne quand il rentre à la maison après son travail.**

(30 seconds)

(t) **Question number two.**

How much does she usually get? Tick the correct box.

(f) **D'habitude, je reçois dix-huit euros par semaine.**

(30 seconds)

(t) **Question number three.**

What does she do to earn her pocket money?

Tick the **three** correct boxes.

(f) **Pour ça, j'aide à la maison. Je dois faire la vaisselle le soir après le dîner, ranger ma chambre, et aussi laver la voiture le week-end.**

(30 seconds)

(t) **Question number four.**

Marie tells you about a part-time job she has.

What does she say? Complete the sentences.

(f) **Je travaille le week-end et le jeudi soir dans un petit supermarché. C'est assez intéressant. Je remplis les rayons, j'aide les clients à trouver les articles qu'ils cherchent, et, ce que j'aime le plus, je travaille à la caisse.**

(30 seconds)

(t) Question number five.

Marie tells you about her free time.

What does she do? Mention **two** things.

(f) **Avec mon job et mes devoirs, je n'ai pas beaucoup de temps libre, mais j'aime regarder les émissions sur la nature à la télé, et j'aime bien faire des promenades sur la plage près de chez moi.**

(30 seconds)

(t) Question number six.

You decide to go out.

Where does Marie suggest that you go? Why does she suggest going there?

(f) **Alors, ce soir on va sortir. Tu veux aller au club des jeunes? Là, tu peux rencontrer mes copains.**

(30 seconds)

(t) Question number seven.

When you get there you meet Jean-Claude. He introduces himself, and asks you some questions.

What does he ask you? Tick **three** boxes.

(m) **Salut! Je m'appelle Jean-Claude. Bienvenue en France! Quand es-tu arrivé? Combien de temps vas-tu rester ici? Tu as déjà visité cette région de la France?**

(30 seconds)

(t) Question number eight.

You go to a cafe. What does Jean-Claude order?

Mention **three** things.

(m) **Deux sandwiches au jambon, une glace au chocolat, et trois cocas, s'il vous plaît, Madame.**

(30 seconds)

(t) Question number nine.

He tells you that he is going on holiday to Finland soon.

What does he say? Write **T** (True) or **F** (False) in the boxes below.

(m) **Dans dix jours, je pars en vacances en Finlande avec mes parents—pour six semaines! On va loger chez mon oncle et ma tante qui habitent là-bas. Ce sera formidable!**

(30 seconds)

[Turn over for Questions 10 to 12 on *Page four*

(t) Question number ten.

He tells you how they will be travelling.

Why are they going by plane? Give **two** reasons.

(m) Mon père a décidé qu'on va y aller en avion. Le voyage en voiture serait beaucoup trop long et fatigant.

(*30 seconds*)

(t) Question number eleven.

It is time to go home.

What does Marie have to do for her mother on the way home?

(f) Tiens! Il est quatre heures déjà! Il faut rentrer à la maison, mais d'abord je dois acheter des fleurs au marché pour Maman.

(*30 seconds*)

(t) Question number twelve.

Why has her mother asked her to do this?

(f) Maman va voir une copine qui est malade. Elle est à l'hôpital depuis une semaine.

(*30 seconds*)

(t) End of test.

Now look over your answers.

[*END OF TRANSCRIPT*]

FOR OFFICIAL USE

G

Total Mark

1000/406

NATIONAL QUALIFICATIONS 2003

WEDNESDAY, 14 MAY
1.45 PM – 2.10 PM
(APPROX)

FRENCH
STANDARD GRADE
General Level
Listening

Fill in these boxes and read what is printed below.

Full name of centre

Town

Forename(s)

Surname

Date of birth
Day Month Year

Scottish candidate number

Number of seat

When you are told to do so, open your paper.

You will hear a number of short items in French. You will hear each item three times, then you will have time to write your answer.

Write your answers, **in English**, in this book, in the appropriate spaces.

You may take notes as you are listening to the French, but only in this paper.

You may **not** use a French dictionary.

You are not allowed to leave the examination room until the end of the test.

Before leaving the examination room you must give this book to the invigilator. If you do not, you may lose all the marks for this paper.

SCOTTISH QUALIFICATIONS AUTHORITY
©

THB 1000/406 6/45670

DO NO
WRITE
THIS
MARGI

Marks

You are on holiday in France. You are spending a fortnight with your French pen-friend, Marie.

Vous êtes en vacances en France. Vous passez une quinzaine chez votre correspondante française, Marie.

1. Marie talks to you about pocket money.

(*a*) When does Marie get her pocket money? **1**

____

(*b*) Who does she get her pocket money from? **1**

____

* * * * *

2. How much does she usually get? Tick (✓) the correct box. **1**

8€		10€		18€	

* * * * *

3. What does she do to earn her pocket money? Tick (✓) the **three** correct boxes. **3**

 ☐

 ☐

 ☐

 ☐

 ☐

 ☐

* * * * *

DO NOT WRITE IN THIS MARGIN

Marks

4. Marie tells you about a part-time job she has.

What does she say? Complete the sentences. **3**

Marie works in a ____________________ . She helps the customers to

____________________ and she also ____________________ .

* * * * *

5. Marie tells you about her free time.

What does she do? Mention **two** things. **2**

____

____

* * * * *

6. You decide to go out.

(*a*) Where does Marie suggest that you go? **1**

____

(*b*) Why does she suggest going there? **1**

____

* * * * *

7. When you get there you meet Jean-Claude. He introduces himself, and asks you some questions.

What does he ask you? Tick (✓) **three** boxes. **3**

When did you arrive?	
Did you arrive yesterday?	
How long are you here for?	
Is this your first visit to France?	
Have you been to this part of France before?	
Do you like this part of France?	

* * * * *

[Turn over for Questions 8 to 12 on *Page four*

DO NOT WRITE IN THIS MARGIN

Marks

8. You go to a cafe. What does Jean-Claude order?
Mention **three** things. **3**

____

____

____

* * * * *

9. He tells you that he is going on holiday to Finland soon.
What does he say? Write **T** (True) or **F** (False) in the boxes below. **3**

He is leaving in twelve days.	
He is going for six weeks.	
His aunt and uncle are taking him.	

* * * * *

10. He tells you how they will be travelling.

Why are they going by plane? Give **two** reasons. **2**

____

____

* * * * *

11. It is time to go home.

What does Marie have to do for her mother on the way home? **1**

____

* * * * *

12. Why has her mother asked her to do this? **1**

____

* * * * *

Total (26)

[*END OF QUESTION PAPER*]

2004 GENERAL

FOR OFFICIAL USE

G

Total

1000/402

NATIONAL QUALIFICATIONS 2004

TUESDAY, 11 MAY
10.05 AM – 10.50 AM

FRENCH
STANDARD GRADE
General Level
Reading

Fill in these boxes and read what is printed below.

Full name of centre

Town

Forename(s)

Surname

Date of birth
Day Month Year

Scottish candidate number

Number of seat

When you are told to do so, open your paper and write your answers **in English** in the spaces provided.

You may use a French dictionary.

Before leaving the examination room you must give this book to the invigilator. If you do not, you may lose all the marks for this paper.

SCOTTISH QUALIFICATIONS AUTHORITY ©

Marks

You are reading a French magazine.

1. Some primary school pupils give their opinions about school.

Que penses-tu de l'école?

Moi, j'aime aller à l'école pour les copains. La maîtresse est gentille, mais ce que je préfère vraiment, c'est la récréation!

Guillaume, 8 ans

J'aime ma maîtresse. Elle explique très bien et j'apprends beaucoup de choses avec elle. J'aime bien l'école, mais mon Papa et ma Maman me manquent.

Jacqueline, 9 ans

A l'école, je préfère le calcul et l'histoire. Mais, parfois, c'est fatigant aussi. J'aimerais avoir des consoles et des jeux-vidéo.

Paulette, 10 ans

Je n'aime pas l'école parce que je n'aime pas travailler. C'est ennuyeux. Je préfère rester chez moi, jouer avec mon chien.

Jean-Luc, 8 ans

Which of the pupils said the following? **3**

Sometimes school is tiring. ______________________

What I really like is the morning break. ______________________

I'd rather stay at home. ______________________

DO NOT WRITE IN THIS MARGIN

Marks

2. On the letters page of the magazine, you see this letter from a girl.

Je l'aime, comment lui dire?

Salut! Je veux bien inviter un garçon de ma classe à sortir avec moi. Mais je suis très timide, et j'ai peur de lui parler.
Je l'aime tellement. Aide-moi! Que dois-je faire?

Adrienne

(*a*) What does Adrienne want to do? **1**

____

____

(*b*) Why does she find this difficult?
Mention any **one** thing. **1**

____

3. Then you read the advice given to the girl.

Conseil

Chère Adrienne!

Il y a beaucoup de filles qui sont comme toi. A ton âge, c'est normal. Tu peux commencer en lui parlant des choses que vous avez en commun, comme les devoirs, les jeux-vidéo que tu préfères etc.

Complete the sentences. **2**

She is told that many girls ____________________________.

She should talk to him about ____________________________

____.

[Turn over

DO NOT WRITE IN THIS MARGIN

Marks

4. On another page of the magazine, you read some rules you should stick to when babysitting.

La Loi du Babysitter

Quand on garde des enfants, il ne faut jamais.........

- ......laisser un enfant seul
- ......utiliser le téléphone de la famille pour ses appels personnels
- ......inviter son petit copain
- ......fumer devant les enfants.

Complete the sentences. **4**

You must never:

leave a child ______________________________.

use ______________________________.

invite ______________________________.

smoke ______________________________.

DO NOT WRITE IN THIS MARGIN

Marks

5. There is an article in the magazine about Harry Potter.

La Naissance de Harry Potter

Joanne Kathleen Rowling est née en Angleterre en 1967. Sa mère travaillait dans une bibliothèque, donc la petite Joanne lisait beaucoup.

Un jour, elle voyage en chemin de fer entre Manchester et Londres quand l'idée lui vient d'écrire l'histoire d'un petit sorcier nommé Harry.

Plus tard, en travaillant au Portugal, elle écrit trois chapitres du premier livre "Harry Potter".

Elle revient vivre à Edimbourg, en Ecosse, où elle termine son livre. Elle l'envoie à des agents littéraires, mais ils le refusent. Après un an, elle trouve un éditeur qui veut bien le publier.

Mais le succès n'est pas instantané; ce n'est qu'avec la parution du troisième livre que les aventures de Harry deviennent célèbres partout dans le monde et que J. K. Rowling fait sa fortune.

(*a*) Why did J. K. Rowling read a lot when she was a child? **1**

____

(*b*) Where did she first have the idea of writing about Harry? **1**

____

(*c*) What did she do in Portugal? **1**

____

(*d*) Why did it take so long for the book to appear?
Give any **one** reason. **1**

____

(*e*) What happened when the third book appeared?
Mention **two** things. **2**

____

____

[Turn over

DO NOT WRITE IN THIS MARGIN

Marks

6. You read about a new use for the Internet.

L'Internet à l'Hôpital

Tous les jours, il y a 150 000 enfants à l'hôpital en France. Bien sûr, ils sont malades, mais souvent, ils souffrent aussi de l'isolement.

Maintenant, plusieurs hôpitaux ont installé des ordinateurs et des liaisons Internet. Comme ça, les enfants restent en contact avec leur école et peuvent communiquer avec leurs copains.

En général, les médecins sont pour cette idée, car ça permet aux enfants de guérir plus vite.

(*a*) When children are ill in hospital, what other problem do they often have? **1**

(*b*) How does having access to the Internet help the children? **2**

(*c*) Why are doctors in favour of this use of the Internet? **1**

DO NOT WRITE IN THIS MARGIN

Marks

7. One day, your pen pal's sister shows you a letter she has written to a hotel in England.

Fabienne GARNIER,
16, rue des Rosiers,
45360 MONTCLAIR,
France

Royal Hotel,
LEICESTER
Angleterre

Monsieur,

J'ai lu sur votre site web que vous cherchez un(e) jeune Français(e) pour travailler dans votre hôtel pendant les mois de juillet et d'août.

J'ai 19 ans et, pendant mes vacances scolaires, j'ai déjà travaillé dans un petit hôtel ici à Montclair. Dans ce travail, j'ai souvent parlé avec des touristes britanniques.

Je voudrais bien passer quelques mois en Grande-Bretagne pour perfectionner mon anglais et me renseigner sur les différences entre les hôtels français et les hôtels britanniques.

Je vous prie d'agréer, Monsieur, mes sincères salutations.

Fabienne Garnier

(*a*) What has Fabienne done previously during her school holidays? **1**

(*b*) How has this prepared her for working in Great Britain? **1**

(*c*) Why does she want to spend time in Great Britain? **2**

[Turn over

DO NOT WRITE IN THIS MARGIN

Marks

8. In a newspaper, you read this article about a young driver.

Attention! Petite au volant!

Dans la ville de Sydney, en Australie, une petite fille de huit ans a décidé de conduire la voiture de sa mère.

La voiture était dans le parking d'un supermarché où sa mère faisait des courses.

La petite voulait rentrer à la maison toute seule dans la voiture.

Heureusement, après quelques centaines de mètres, un policier a réussi à arrêter la voiture.

Tick (✓) **True** or **False** for each sentence. **4**

	True	False
An eight-year-old girl was driving a car.		
Her mother had given her the keys.		
Her mother was shopping at the time.		
The girl drove into a police car.		

DO NOT WRITE IN THIS MARGIN

Marks

9. On another page, you read an unusual story about a postcard.

E-MAIL – QUELQUES SECONDES

POSTE – SOIXANTE-TREIZE ANS

Grâce à l'Internet, un message électronique met quelques secondes à parcourir la planète.

Ce n'est pas le cas d'une certaine carte postale. Envoyée il y a soixante-treize ans, elle est arrivée à sa destination cette année au mois de février.

Malheureusement, la destinataire est morte. Mais sa fille, qui habite toujours la même adresse, a reçu la carte.

Complete the sentences. **3**

An electronic message takes only a few seconds to ______________________

____.

The postcard was sent ____.

The person it was sent to has died, but her daughter received the card

because ____.

Total (32)

[*END OF QUESTION PAPER*]

[BLANK PAGE]

G

1000/407

NATIONAL QUALIFICATIONS 2004

TUESDAY, 11 MAY
1.45 PM – 2.10 PM
(APPROX)

FRENCH STANDARD GRADE

General Level
Listening Transcript

This paper must not be seen by any candidate.

The material overleaf is provided for use in an emergency only (eg the recording or equipment proving faulty) or where permission has been given in advance by SQA for the material to be read to candidates with special needs. The material must be read exactly as printed.

SCOTTISH QUALIFICATIONS AUTHORITY

Transcript—General Level

Instructions to reader(s): For each item, read the English **once**, then read the French **three times**, with an interval of 5 seconds between the readings. On completion of the third reading, pause for the length of time indicated in brackets after each item, to allow the candidates to write their answers. Where special arrangements have been agreed in advance to allow the reading of the material, those sections marked **(f)** should be read by a female speaker and those marked **(m)** by a male: those sections marked **(t)** should be read by the teacher.

(t) You are spending two weeks at the home of your French pen pal, Julie.

(m) or (f) Tu passes des vacances chez ta correspondante française, Julie.

(t) Question number one.

When you arrive, Julie's father speaks to you.

What does he ask you? Tick **three** boxes.

(m) **Tu es fatigué après ton voyage? Tu vas passer combien de temps ici? Tu as déjà visité la France?**

(*30 seconds*)

(t) Question number two.

Julie tells you about the plans for tomorrow.

What will you be doing? Complete the sentences.

(f) **Demain, on va passer la journée en ville. Tu sais, le samedi matin, il y a un marché sur la place. L'après-midi, on va au centre sportif voir mes copains.**

(*30 seconds*)

(t) Question number three.

Julie talks about someone she wants you to meet during your stay.

Who is this person? What is he organising?

(f) **Je dois te présenter à mon professeur d'anglais. Il organise un voyage scolaire pour nous. On va visiter le sud de l'Angleterre.**

(*30 seconds*)

(t) Question number four.

Julie's dad tells you he works for a shop which sells electrical goods.

What exactly does he do? Tick **one** box.

(m) **Je ne travaille pas dans le magasin. Quand un client achète une nouvelle machine à laver ou un nouveau frigo, moi, je vais chez le client pour installer la machine.**

(*30 seconds*)

(t) Question number five.

He tells you more about his job.

Why does he like it? Mention **two** things.

(m) C'est bien parce qu'on rencontre beaucoup de gens, et ce que j'aime le plus, c'est que je travaille seul.

(30 seconds)

(t) Question number six.

Julie says you will be going to a football match at the weekend.

Who is playing?

(f) Ça va être passionnant. C'est un match entre deux équipes de première division.

(30 seconds)

(t) Question number seven.

Julie tells you about the football stadium.

Tick **True** or **False** for each sentence.

(f) C'est un stade très moderne, près de la ville. Il y a des places pour trente mille spectateurs et un parking énorme derrière le stade.

(30 seconds)

(t) Question number eight.

She tells you about the tickets for the match.

When did her dad buy them? How much did they cost?

(f) En France, les matchs de foot coûtent cher. Mon père a acheté les billets la semaine dernière. Il a payé quarante euros le billet.

(30 seconds)

(t) Question number nine.

Julie then tells you what you will be doing in the second week of your stay.

Complete the sentences.

(f) On va passer une semaine chez ma tante. Elle habite à la montagne, près de la frontière espagnole.

(30 seconds)

[Turn over for Questions 10 to 12 on *Page four*

(t) Question number ten.

Julie talks about the journey there.

How long will it take? Why will you travel by car?

(f) Pour y aller, ça fait cinq heures et demie de route. Mais la voiture est pratique parce que nous avons beaucoup de bagages.

(*30 seconds*)

(t) Question number eleven.

You will have several stops during your journey.

Why? Give any **one** reason.

(f) On va s'arrêter plusieurs fois pendant le voyage. Ma petite soeur n'aime pas tellement les voyages en voiture. Souvent, elle se sent malade.

(*30 seconds*)

(t) Question number twelve.

Julie talks about the things you can do while you are there.

What can you do there? Mention any **three** things.

(f) A la montagne, on peut faire de l'escalade, bien sûr. Mais on peut aussi faire des promenades à pied, et à cheval. Il y a même un petit lac où on peut faire de la voile.

(*30 seconds*)

(t) End of test.

Now look over your answers.

[*END OF TRANSCRIPT*]

FOR OFFICIAL USE

G

Total Mark

1000/406

NATIONAL QUALIFICATIONS 2004

TUESDAY, 11 MAY
1.45 PM – 2.10 PM
(APPROX)

FRENCH
STANDARD GRADE
General Level
Listening

Fill in these boxes and read what is printed below.

Full name of centre

Town

Forename(s)

Surname

Date of birth
Day Month Year

Scottish candidate number

Number of seat

When you are told to do so, open your paper.

You will hear a number of short items in French. You will hear each item three times, then you will have time to write your answer.

Write your answers, **in English**, in this book, in the appropriate spaces.

You may take notes as you are listening to the French, but only in this paper.

You may **not** use a French dictionary.

You are not allowed to leave the examination room until the end of the test.

Before leaving the examination room you must give this book to the invigilator. If you do not, you may lose all the marks for this paper.

DO NOT WRITE IN THIS MARGIN

Marks

You are spending two weeks at the home of your French pen pal, Julie.

Tu passes des vacances chez ta correspondante française, Julie.

1. When you arrive, Julie's father speaks to you. What does he ask you? Tick (✓) **three** boxes. **3**

Are you tired after your journey?	
How long are you staying?	
How long was your journey?	
How do you like France?	
Have you been to France before?	
Are you hungry?	

* * * * *

2. Julie tells you about the plans for tomorrow. What will you be doing? Complete the sentences. **3**

You will be spending the day ______________________________.

In the morning there is a ______________________________.

In the afternoon, you will go to the sports centre to ______________________________

______________________________.

* * * * *

3. Julie talks about someone she wants you to meet during your stay.

(*a*) Who is this person? **1**

____

(*b*) What is he organising? **1**

____

* * * * *

DO NOT WRITE IN THIS MARGIN

Marks

4. Julie's dad tells you he works for a shop which sells electrical goods. What exactly does he do? Tick (✓) **one** box. **1**

He sells washing machines and fridges to customers.	
He installs washing machines and fridges in customers' homes.	
He repairs washing machines and fridges for customers.	

* * * * *

5. He tells you more about his job. Why does he like it? Mention **two** things. **2**

____

____

* * * * *

6. Julie says you will be going to a football match at the weekend. Who is playing? **1**

____

* * * * *

7. Julie tells you about the football stadium. Tick (✓) **True** or **False** for each sentence. **3**

	True	**False**
The stadium is in the town centre.		
It holds 50,000 spectators.		
There is a large car park behind the stadium.		

* * * * *

[Turn over for Questions 8 to 12 on *Page four*

DO NOT WRITE IN THIS MARGIN

Marks

8. She tells you about the tickets for the match.

(*a*) When did her dad buy them? 1

____

(*b*) How much did they cost? 1

____

* * * * *

9. Julie then tells you what you will be doing in the second week of your stay. Complete the sentences. 3

You will spend a week at ____________________________

in the ________________, near the ________________ border.

* * * * *

10. Julie talks about the journey there.

(*a*) How long will it take? 1

____

(*b*) Why will you travel by car? 1

____

* * * * *

11. You will have several stops during your journey. Why? Give any **one** reason. 1

____

* * * * *

12. Julie talks about the things you can do while you are there. What can you do there? Mention any **three** things. 3

____

____

____

* * * * *

Total (26)

[*END OF QUESTION PAPER*]